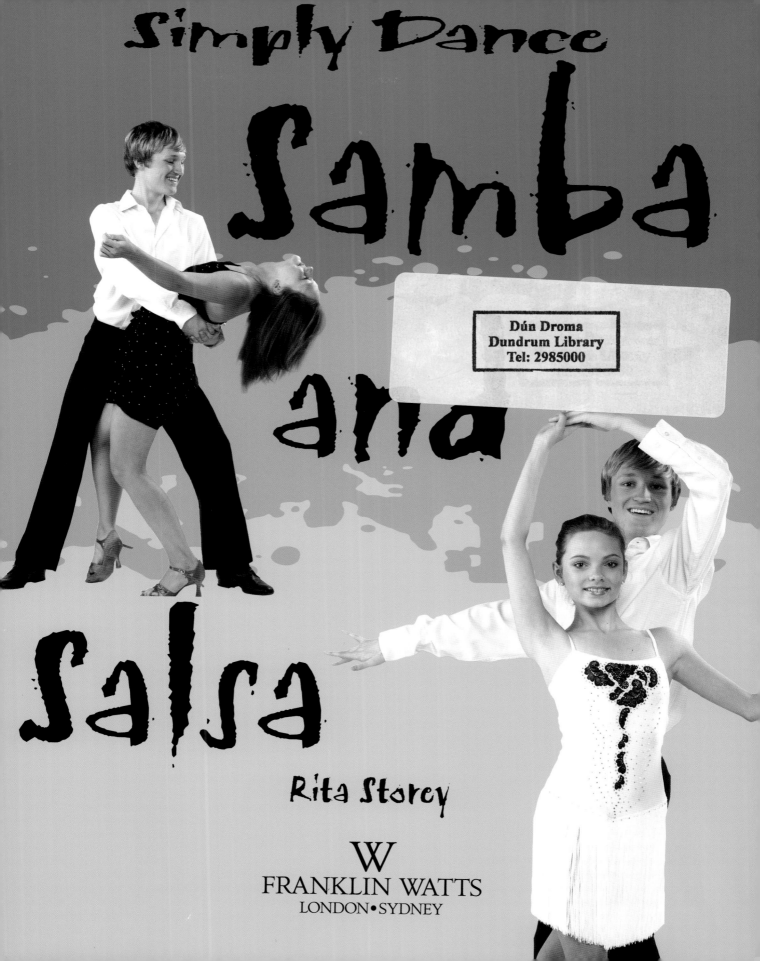

Simply Dance

Samba

and

Salsa

Rita Storey

W
FRANKLIN WATTS
LONDON • SYDNEY

Before you start

Dancing is a great way to get fit and to meet people. Wherever you live there are likely to be dance classes held somewhere nearby. There are some steps in this book that you can try to get you started. There are also some suggestions for clips of music to listen to on pages 28 and 29.

You do not need a special costume to learn to dance. A pair of comfortable shoes and clothes that let you move easily will be fine to start with. It is not a good idea to wear trainers when you are dancing as the soles grip the floor and make it difficult to turn your feet easily. Some dance studios have their own dress code, so you might want to check what it is before turning up to a class.

When you are dancing it is a good idea to wear two or three thin layers of clothing. At the start of a dance session you need to keep your muscles warm to avoid damaging them when you stretch. As you get warmer you can take off some layers.

Like any type of physical exercise, dance has an element of risk. It is advisable to consult a healthcare professional before beginning any programme of exercise, particularly if you are overweight or suffer from any medical conditions. Before you begin, prepare your body with a few gentle stretches and exercises to warm you up.

Dancing is getting more and more popular. Give it a try and find out why!

First published in 2010 by
Franklin Watts
338 Euston Road
London NW1 3BH

Franklin Watts Australia
Level 17/207 Kent Street
Sydney NSW 2000

© Franklin Watts 2010
Series editor: Sarah Peutrill
Art director: Jonathan Hair

Series designed and created for
Franklin Watts by Storeybooks
Designer: Rita Storey
Editor: Nicola Barber
Photography: Tudor Photography

A CIP catalogue record for this book is available
from the British Library

Printed in China

Dewey classification: 793.3'3
ISBN 978 0 7496 9364 0

Picture credits
All photographs Tudor Photography, Banbury
unless otherwise stated
© Photos 12 / Alamy p15, © Alex Segre / Alamy
p27; Bigstock p29; i-stock pp 5,14 and 17;
Shutterstock pp 5 and 28; ABC/Everett/Rex
Features p26
Cover images Tudor Photography

All photos posed by models. Thanks to Ryan
Brown, Jake Thomas Chawner, Lauren Cooper,
Amy Kennedy and Libby Williams

The Publisher would like to thank dance adviser
Kate Fisher (www.katefisherdanceacademy.com)
for her invaluable help and support.

Franklin Watts is a division of Hachette Children's
Books, an Hachette UK company.
www.hachette.co.uk

Contents

Ballroom dances

Samba and salsa

Ballroom dances are performed by couples and recognised in competitions around the world. They are split into two groups: 'International Latin' and 'International Standard'. Latin dances usually have a lot of hip action and rhythmic expression. They do not always have to be danced in a **closed hold** (with both hands in contact). The couple may dance side-by-side, or even dance different moves from each other. In International Standard ballroom dancing, a couple must remain in a closed hold for most of the dance.

The samba and salsa are both happy and energetic Latin dances. As well as being a partner dance, salsa is also danced solo and in groups.

What is the samba?

The samba is a style of music and dance that originated in Brazil. It is popular all over the world, but it is most famous for being the music and dance of the spectacular carnivals held in Rio de Janeiro.

In the early 1500s many Portuguese people moved to Brazil and set up sugar plantations. The Portuguese needed workers for their plantations, so they brought captives from West Africa to work as slaves. It is widely believed that the origins of the samba are the traditional tribal dances and music brought to Brazil by the African slaves. Dancing was a way for the slaves to forget the miseries of their everyday lives for a while.

International samba

In the 1920s Rio de Janero in Brazil was a popular place for tourists to visit. Many tourists learned the samba and then took the dance back to Europe and the USA.

By the 1930s the samba was very popular, especially in the USA. At this time the various different forms of samba were standardised into an internationally recognised dance.

Once they have mastered the basic samba steps dancers can have fun with more advanced moves, such as this shoulder shimmy.

The international form of the samba is a partner dance which retains the carnival atmosphere but with standard rhythm and steps. Other more traditional forms of the samba, such as **Batucada** and **Maracatu**, are danced at carnivals and Mardi Gras.

A spectacular headdress is an important part of a samba dancer's Mardi Gras costume.

Mardi Gras

Carnivals are held in many different places around the world. In Brazil the carnival of Mardi Gras ('Fat Tuesday') lasts for six days and is the most spectacular of them all. Carnival means 'goodbye to meat'. The party starts on Shrove Tuesday. This is the day in the Christian calendar when people traditionally ate up all the meat in the house in preparation for Lent, the 40 days of prayer and fasting that lead up to Easter.

Today, Mardi Gras is an explosion of colour, dance and music. At its centre is a parade of floats with samba dancers and musicians. Hundreds of samba schools (*escolas de samba*) compete against each other to be judged the best in the parade. The schools spend all year preparing for Mardi Gras: finding a theme, choreographing dances and making the costumes. There is a panel of judges who award points for the musicians, the dancers, the floats and the costumes.

Samba — the basics

The samba has some travelling steps **and some steps that are danced almost on the spot. The dance is quick and light, and its character** comes from the rhythmic bounce action of the feet and knees as you dance the steps. **The combination of the bounce action and steps, as well as arm movements and hip action, makes the samba a** tricky dance to learn.

one

Natural basic

'a'

two

Start with your weight on your left foot.

Start with your weight on your right foot.

1 Step forwards on to your right foot.

1 Step back on to your left foot.

2 Transfer your weight back on to your right foot.

2 Transfer your weight back on to your left foot.

a Close left foot to right foot and shift your weight on to the ball of your left foot. Do not lower the heel.

a Close right foot to left foot and shift your weight on to the ball of your right foot. Do not lower the heel.

Samba holds

The samba is danced using a Latin closed hold. The boy's right hand is on the girl's left shoulder blade. The girl's left hand is on the boy's right shoulder. Their other hands are clasped. The girl is slightly to the right of the boy. The hold is close but there is no body contact.

Samba basic steps

Two of the basic steps in the samba are the natural and the progressive. The rhythm of a samba varies. To avoid confusion all the steps explained on pages 6–11 are done to the same rhythm. This is counted as: 1 'a' 2 3 'a' 4. Count 1 'a' 2 3 'a' 4 as you dance the moves.

This couple are in a Latin closed hold, ready to dance the samba.

three

3 Step back with your left foot.

3 Step forwards with your right foot.

'a'

a Close right foot to left foot and shift your weight on to the ball of your right foot. Do not lower the heel.

a Close left foot to right foot and shift your weight on to the ball of your left foot. Do not lower the heel.

four

4 Transfer your weight back on to your left foot.

4 Transfer your weight back on to your right foot.

Samba steps

It is important to get the feel of the samba rhythms when you are learning these steps. There are suggestions for music to listen to, as well as clips to watch, on page 28. You can practise the basic steps with or without a partner.

on page 28

Progressive basic

one

'a'

two

Begin with your knees slightly bent.

Bend your knees as you transfer your weight.

1 Step forwards on to your right foot.

1 Step back on to your left foot.

2 Transfer your weight back on to your right foot.

2 Transfer your weight back on to your left foot.

Straighten your legs slightly as you close your feet.

a Close left foot to right foot. Transfer your weight on to the ball of your left foot.

a Close right foot to left foot. Transfer your weight on to the ball of your right foot.

The samba bounce action

Once you have mastered the basic steps the next thing you need to do is add 'bounce'. This shouldn't be exaggerated, but adding the bounce to the knees and feet allows you to introduce the third element – the hip action. This should follow naturally as you bend and straighten your legs.

three

'a'

four

3 Step to the side with your left foot.

3 Step to the side with your right foot.

4 Transfer your weight back on to your left foot.

4 Transfer your weight back on to your right foot.

Bend your knees as you transfer your weight.

Straighten your legs slightly as you step to the side.

a Close right foot to left foot. Transfer your weight on to the ball of your right foot.

a Close left foot to right foot. Transfer your weight on to the ball of your left foot.

Samba whisk to the right

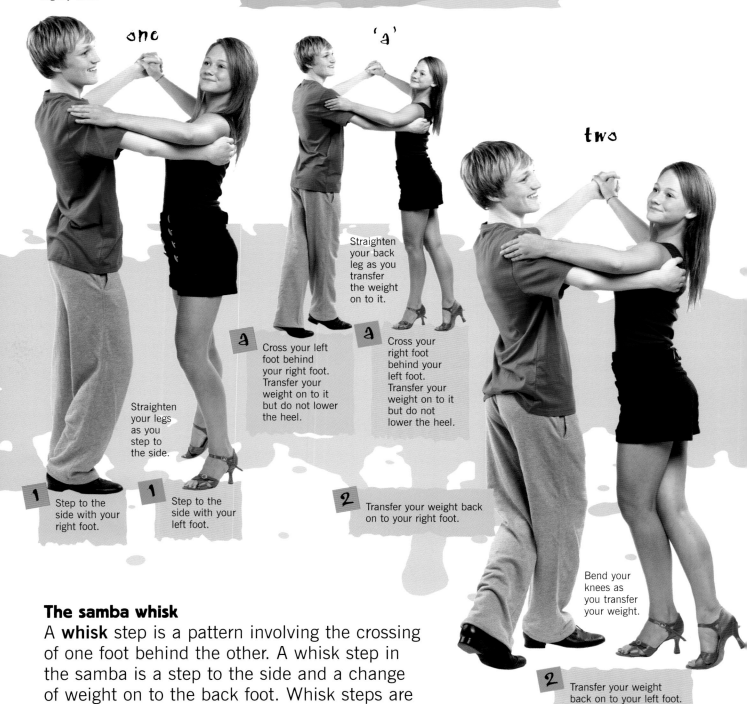

one

'a'

two

Straighten
your back
leg as you
transfer
the weight
on to it.

a Cross your left
foot behind
your right foot.
Transfer your
weight on to it
but do not lower
the heel.

a Cross your
right foot
behind your
left foot.
Transfer your
weight on to it
but do not
lower the heel.

Straighten
your legs
as you
step to
the side.

1 Step to the
side with your
right foot.

1 Step to the
side with your
left foot.

2 Transfer your weight back
on to your right foot.

Bend your
knees as
you transfer
your weight.

2 Transfer your weight
back on to your left foot.

The samba whisk

A **whisk** step is a pattern involving the crossing
of one foot behind the other. A whisk step in
the samba is a step to the side and a change
of weight on to the back foot. Whisk steps are
danced in other dances as well as the samba.

Samba whisk with underarm turn

To do a samba whisk with an underarm turn
the boy does not need to change his steps.

one

Samba whisk to the left

'a'

two

Straighten your legs as you step to the side.

1 Step to the side with your left foot.

1 Step to the side with your right foot.

Straighten your back leg as you transfer the weight on to it.

a Cross your right foot behind your left foot. Transfer your weight on to it but do not lower the heel.

a Cross your left foot behind your right foot. Transfer your weight on to it but do not lower the heel.

Bend your knees as you transfer your weight.

2 Transfer your weight back on to your left foot.

2 Transfer your weight back on to your right foot.

He dances a whisk to the left and to the right – to the left and to the right. The girl does a whisk to the left, then she takes her hand off the boy's shoulder and turns anticlockwise under his raised arm while he dances a whisk to the right. On the next **beat** she is back in hold to start the sequence again.

Putting it all together

The dance steps on pages 6–11 can be joined together to make a routine if you follow the sequence shown below.

Natural basic (pages 6–7)

Start with your feet together, weight on the left foot (boy), right foot (girl).

one 'a' two three 'a' four

Progressive basic (pages 8–9)

one 'a' two three 'a' four

Once you know the steps, add the samba bounce action and a happy carnival feel – then you are on your way to learning to dance the samba.

Samba whisk to the right (page 10)

one   'a'   two

1   a   2

Samba whisk to the left (page 11)

one   'a'   two

1   a   2

Start the **routine** again from the beginning.

Competition samba

Ballroom dancing is a great way to keep fit and have fun. As dancers improve they often like to enter competitions to see how well they can perform against each other. Couples take part in ballroom dance competitions locally, nationally and internationally. If they win they may take home a cup or a prize, but for those who do not there is still the enjoyment of mixing with other dancers and making new friends – as well as the excitement of performing in front of an audience.

Judging the International Latin samba

In the samba the judges are looking for a carnival dance. They expect lots of hip action and bounce in the steps, as well as expressive arm movements and fast **footwork**. They judge the technical performance of the dance steps and the style of the performance.

Samba costumes

Girls wear short dresses for most of the Latin dances to show off their fast footwork and hip movements. The costumes reflect the style of the dance. They may be decorated with sequins, **rhinestones**, beads, jewels, fringes and feathers. Fringes show off the dancers' shoulder and

Make-up and costumes help to create the right image for each Latin dance. They are an important part of samba dancing competitions.

hip movements, and jewels and sequins catch the light to add even more sparkle to the dance.

Men's Latin outfits are tight-fitting to accentuate their moves. Some men wear plain black as a contrast to the girls' brightly coloured dresses. Couples who dance together regularly have costumes made to match.

Competition steps

As an International Latin dance, the samba has a syllabus of steps from which a choreographer can choose when making up a routine. This samba roll **(left)** is one of the more advanced steps a choreographer can use. Putting together a spectacular dance sequence that shows off what the dancers can do is an important part of winning competitions.

Samba on stage and in the movies

In the 1920s, a Broadway play called *Street Carnival* gave the audience in the USA its first taste of samba music and dance. But it was in the following decades that the samba was at its most popular. The movie *Flying Down to Rio* (1933) starred Fred Astaire and Ginger Rogers and featured the samba. In the 1940s a Brazilian samba singer called Carmen Miranda **(right)** starred in movies such as *That Night in Rio* (1941) and *Copacabana* (1947). She became almost as famous for her spectacular outfits and headdresses as she did for her samba singing and dancing. Her costumes set a new fashion, and the samba dance craze took over the New York City dance halls.

What is the salsa?

The salsa is a Latin American party dance, full of energy and fun. It is danced to salsa music which is vibrant and dynamic. The word salsa means 'sauce' in Spanish.

Salsa rhythms

Salsa music began in Cuba as a combination of African-Caribbean and Latin rhythms known as **Son**. Other dances, including the cha-cha, rumba, merengue and mambo, developed from Son, and there are many similarities between them all. In the late 1950s, many Cuban singers and musicians moved to the USA, particularly to New York City. They fused Son music with Puerto Rican rhythms. The word salsa was invented in the 1970s to describe a whole group of **Latin American** rhythms.

Informal salsa

The salsa dance, like the music it is danced to, is a mixture of different styles. Unlike some other dances, the salsa has never been formalised as a Latin ballroom dance. Salsa is often taught alongside the International Latin dances, but it has retained its own informal character. It has also remained popular as a social dance in salsa clubs around the world.

When salsa is danced in competition the routines are choreographed to include eye-catching moves to impress the judges.

A salsa revival

In the 1980s and 1990s salsa music and dance had a surge of popularity. Latin American singers such as Ricky Martin, Enrique Iglesias and Gloria Estefan made the music modern and popular. People wanted to learn the Latin moves, and salsa classes became very fashionable.

Salsa suelta

Some dance classes teach *salsa suelta* – **solo** salsa. You can learn the steps, rhythms and routines of salsa in a group, without the need for a partner.

Dancing as a group

Rueda de Casino (salsa wheel) is a group dance style of salsa. Couples dance in a circle following moves that are called out or signalled by a caller. It is a difficult version of salsa to learn as there are lots of moves, but it is spectacular to watch.

A *salsa suelta* class in action. You don't need a partner to learn this type of salsa.

Salsa – the basics

The movement in the salsa is mainly in the hips and legs. The leg action creates the hip action. The salsa is less rigidly structured than other Latin dances and there are many different variations.

Steps in salsa are taken mainly on the ball of the foot. The heel is lowered only when the weight is completely transferred.

The salsa action

The salsa action is a way of transferring weight from one leg to the other which moves the hips and creates the look and feel of salsa dancing. Begin by practising this move without a partner.

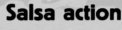

Salsa action

The salsa has a more relaxed hold than the basic Latin hold.

With your legs together, bend your left knee and rest the inside edge of the ball of your left foot lightly on the ground.

Let your arms move naturally as you dance.

Straighten your left leg and put your foot flat on the floor, transferring your weight on to it. Rest the inside edge of the ball of your right foot lightly on the ground. As you do this your hips should rotate and your knees should criss-cross.

Salsa steps

In salsa the term 'basic step' or 'break step' usually refers to a rocking step forwards and backwards.

There are four beats in salsa dancing, but only three steps. The other beat is either a pause or a **tap step**. 1, 2, 3, pause/tap; 5, 6, 7, pause/tap. Beats 4 and 8 are silent.

KEY

G The girl's steps

B The boy's steps

Boy and girl steps

Break step

Begin with your feet together and your weight on your left foot.

Begin with your feet together and your weight on your right foot.

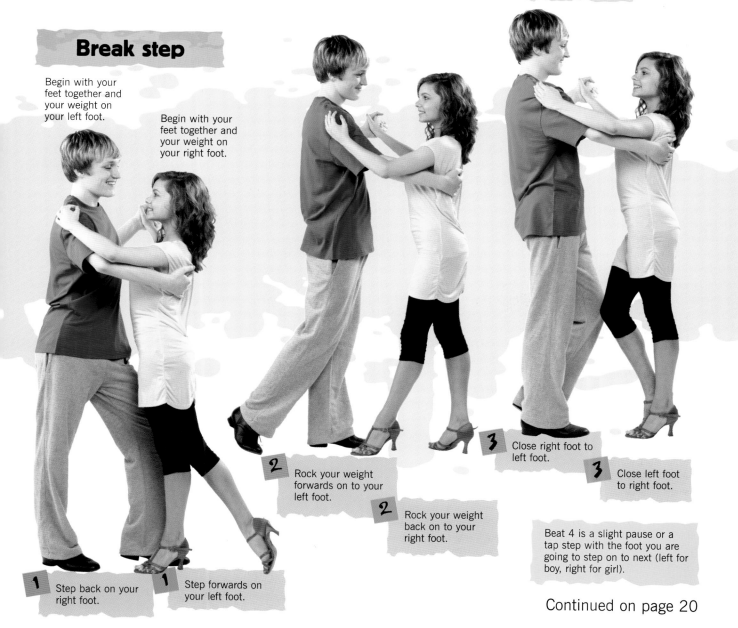

2 Rock your weight forwards on to your left foot.

2 Rock your weight back on to your right foot.

3 Close right foot to left foot.

3 Close left foot to right foot.

Beat 4 is a slight pause or a tap step with the foot you are going to step on to next (left for boy, right for girl).

1 Step back on your right foot.

1 Step forwards on your left foot.

Continued on page 20

Break step (continued)

5 Step forwards on your left foot.

5 Step back on your right foot.

6 Rock weight back on to your right foot.

6 Rock weight forwards on to your left foot.

7 Close left foot to right foot.

7 Close right foot to left foot.

Beat 8 is a slight pause or a tap step with the foot you are going to step on to next (right for boy, left for girl).

Get the salsa beat

It is important to get the feel of the salsa beat when you are practising these steps. Page 29 has suggestions for music you can listen to, as well as clips to watch. Get the beat right and the steps will follow.

Salsa side basic

1 Step to the side with your left foot.

1 Step to the side with your right foot.

2 Transfer your weight back on to your right foot.

2 Transfer your weight back on to your left foot.

3 Close left foot to right foot, straightening your left knee.

3 Close right foot to left foot, straightening your right knee.

Beat 4 is a tap step with the foot you are going to step on to next (right for boy, left for girl).

5 Step to the side with your right foot.

5 Step to the side with your left foot.

6 Transfer your weight back on to your left foot.

6 Transfer your weight back on to your right foot.

7 Close right foot to left foot straightening your right knee.

7 Close left foot to right foot straightening your left knee.

Beat 8 is a tap step with the foot you are going to step on to next (left for boy, right for girl).

More salsa steps

1 Step back on your right foot.

Advanced basic step

Salsa arms
In salsa the arm movements should be natural. Allow your arms to react to your body movements as you dance.

2 Step across your right foot with your left foot.

3 Close right foot to left foot.

Beat 4 Tap your left foot alongside your right foot.

There are so many different versions of salsa that there is no one 'right' way of dancing it. People in different parts of the world have their own salsa music and have created their own dance styles. These include Colombian salsa, Cuban salsa, Miami salsa and **LA (Los Angeles)** salsa.

5 Step back on your left foot.

6 Step across your left foot with your right foot.

7 Close left foot to right foot.

Beat 8 Tap your right foot alongside your left foot.

Putting it all together

The dance steps on pages 19–23 can be joined together to make a routine if you follow the sequence shown below.

Start with your feet together, weight on your left foot (boy), right foot (girl).

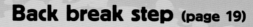

Back break step (page 19)

Pause or tap

Forward break step (page 20)

Pause or tap

Once you know the steps add in some salsa action (see page 18) and a happy party feel and you are on your way to learning to dance the salsa.

Salsa side basic (page 21)

1

2

3

Pause or tap

5

6

7

Advanced basic step (pages 22–3)

Open out to dance side-by-side.

1

2

3

Pause or tap

5

6

7

Pause or tap

Step back into closed hold to start the sequence again.

Competition salsa

Salsa is danced as a social dance in salsa clubs all over the world. The majority of people who learn to dance salsa do so just for the enjoyment of dancing. Many would argue that salsa is about being spontaneous and appreciating the music and dance for its own sake rather than perfecting routines. However, for those who like to have their efforts judged against other people there are competitions run by the World Salsa Federation and Professional Dance Vision International Dance Association.

Learning the steps

The steps and routines are set down in a **syllabus**, which is taught in dance schools. Dancers can take graded exams, called medal tests. In competitions there are categories at all levels for professional and amateur salsa teams, couples and solo dancers.

The judges of a salsa competition look for an energetic party dance. There should be lots of hip action and fast, accurate foot moves. Competitors are judged on their routines, including speed and timing, and their appearance.

Vivica A. Fox and Nick Kosovich perform an energetic salsa move on *Dancing with the Stars*.

Less formal salsa competitions are held in clubs and bars. People usually dress in a fairly relaxed way for these competitions.

Ballroom salsa costumes

The salsa is a fast dance with lots of movement in the feet and legs. Salsa dresses are short to show off the girl's footwork. The costumes reflect the style of the dance and are often in bright party colours. They may also have sequins, rhinestones and beads, or be made of a shimmering fabric. Trousers are sometimes worn by the girls as an alternative to a dress or skirt – usually close-fitting at the hip with flared legs. Men wear trousers and a tight-fitting shirt.

Salsa shine steps

When salsa dancers are confident with the basic steps and rhythms they can add shine steps to their routines. To perform shine steps one of the dancers in a couple breaks away to show off his or her skills in a solo performance.

Dance to the music

Listen carefully to the music you dance to. The regular beat, or pulse, of the music will help you to understand the timing of the steps.

Samba music
Percussion instruments are very important in samba music. They include drums of different sizes and shapes, tambourines, shakers and cow bells. In a carnival the samba band is led by someone blowing a whistle to control the music and dance.

Samba instruments
These are some of the percussion instruments used in a samba band:

agogo: two metal handbells joined together and played by hitting them with a stick.

chocalho: a large, powerful shaker made of wood or metal with a number of steel jingles.

ganza: a long shaker with shells, beads or seeds inside.

pandeiro: a tambourine made of wood and goatskin. It has five sets of jingles.

repinique: a drum with a high, piercing sound.

surdo: a bass drum used to mark time and provide a steady beat. Surdos are the 'heartbeat' of the samba.

timba: a tall drum that makes a low sound when it is hit.

Dance music Samba

A list of samba music can be found on:
www.dancesportmusic.com/samba.html

Short clips for you to listen to:
www.ballroomdancers.com/Music/search_style.asp?Dance=Samba

Other suggestions are:
'Crazy in Love', Beyoncé
'La Isla Bonita', Madonna

Watch this video clip to get you into the samba mood:
http://new.music.yahoo.com/videos/Madonna/La-Isla-Bonita--2144316

Surdo drums being played in a samba band.

Salsa music

Salsa music is difficult to define as a style. Originally salsa music was a mixture of African-Caribbean and Latin rhythms, but it has evolved into many different types of music. Generally, the instruments used in a salsa band include percussion – conga drums, bongos, maracas, **guiro**, **claves** – as well as trombones, trumpets, saxophones, guitars and piano. The exact combination of these instruments will depend on the style of salsa music being played.

Dance to the beat

The essence of all salsa music is its beat, which is called the **clave** (cla-vey). To dance to a clave beat you do not step on the strong (down) beats (as is normal in most dances), you step on the weak beats in-between. If the strong down beats are on one and three, you step on two and four. If the strong down beats are on two and four, you step on one and three.

Dance music salsa

Short clips of traditional salsa music for you to listen to:
www.ballroomdancers.com/Music/search_style.asp?Dance=Salsa

Other suggestions are:-
'Mi Tierra', Gloria Estefan
'Qué Hiciste' (salsa remix), Jennifer Lopez
'Salsa Dance Break', Destiny's Child
'Tu Recuerdo' (salsa version) and 'Vuelve', Ricky Martin

Watch this video clip to get you into the salsa mood:
http://new.music.yahoo.com/videos/GloriaEstefan/Mi-Tierra--2141592

The bongo drums (top and bottom), a guiro (right), and maracas (middle) are all instruments played in salsa bands.

Glossary

Batucada A type of samba danced at carnivals and Mardi Gras.

beat The regular pulse of a piece of music – like a heartbeat or a ticking clock.

caller A person who calls out the movements for dancers to follow.

choreographer The person who arranges the sequence of steps that form a dance.

clave The beat that samba music and samba dances are performed to.

claves A pair of wooden sticks, held one in each hand, that are struck together to accompany music and dancing.

closed hold When a couple dances with the partners facing each other, with both hands in contact. The arm positions are different for each dance.

float A truck carrying a display in a parade.

footwork The way the feet are used in a dance.

guiro A South American musical instrument made from a dried fruit called a gourd. It is played by scraping it with a stick.

International Latin Five Latin dances governed by internationally recognised rules and danced in amateur and professional competitions around the world.

International Standard Five ballroom dances governed by internationally recognised rules and danced in amateur and professional competitions around the world.

Latin American Describes someone or something from the Spanish- or Portuguese-speaking countries of South and Central America.

Maracatu A type of samba danced at carnivals and Mardi Gras.

rhinestone An artificial gem made to look like a diamond.

routine The steps that make up a performance.

samba roll A move in samba dancing in which both partners in a couple stretch forwards and roll their upper bodies in a circle.

shimmy A dance move where the dancer shakes his or her hips or shoulders.

shine step A dance move in which one of a pair of salsa dancers breaks away to show off his or her skills in a solo performance.

solo A performance by one person.

Son The African-Caribbean and Latin rhythms from which salsa developed.

spontaneous Natural and unplanned.

syllabus A summary of all the steps you need to learn for each dance medal or grade.

tap step A dance step where the toe of one foot taps alongside the other foot.

travelling step A step that moves the dance around the floor.

whisk A dance step where one foot is crossed behind the other.

Further information

DVDs

For a taste of ballroom see:
Everything to Dance For (2007)
Mad Hot Ballroom (2005) PG

For classic samba see:
That Night in Rio (1941)

Dance classes

Find a dance class wherever you are in the world!

www.dancesport.uk.com/studios_world/index.htm

DanceSport

Ten ballroom dances are referred to as the DanceSport dances. These dances are governed by internationally recognised rules and are danced in amateur and professional competitions around the world. There are five International Standard and five International Latin dances.

In America the American Smooth and American Rhythm correspond to the International Standard and International Latin classifications.

Websites

All about a samba squad:
www.sambasquad.com/

News from the celebrity TV shows:
abc.go.com/shows/dancing-with-the-stars
www.bbc.co.uk/strictly comedancing/

For short clips of music from each of the samba styles:
www.abanda.dk/Babblefish/samba.htm

Note to parents and teachers

Every effort has been made by the Publishers to ensure that these websites are suitable for children, that they are of the highest educational value, and that they contain no inappropriate or offensive material. However, because of the nature of the Internet, it is impossible to guarantee that the contents of these sites will not be altered. We strongly advise that Internet access is supervised by a responsible adult.

Index